SHANGHAI

上海市人民政府新闻办公室编

上海辞书出版社出版

COMPILED BY INFORMATION OFFICE OF SHANGHAI MUNICIPALITY

PUBLISHED BY SHANGHAI LEXICOGRAPHIC PUBLISHING HOUSE

第3版

上海市市标

The emblem of Shanghai

上海地区卫星遥感图
A satellite view of Shanghai

上海市市花白玉兰
Magnolia, the city flower

前　言

　　上海——这座太平洋西海岸重要的港口城市，正以其神话般的故事引来世界的注目。

　　岁月悠悠，沧海桑田。上海，这个闻名于世的大都市曾是诞生于黄浦江畔的一个小渔村。历史上的上海，曾凭藉位居中国黄金海岸与黄金水道交汇点这一得天独厚的区位优势，逐步发展成为远东地区著名的金融贸易中心和近代文明的大都市。历史上称其为"江海通津，东南都会。"勤劳的上海人民曾挥洒时间的巨笔，饱蘸黄浦江水写下上海历史灿烂的一页。

　　然而，更为辉煌的记录还是在今天。当人类进入 20 世纪 90 年代，历史再一次垂青于这座城市，改革开放使上海呈现出一片生机勃勃的景象：新建的南浦、杨浦、奉浦、徐浦大桥横跨浦江之上，气势雄伟，蔚为壮观；三条江底隧道宛如火龙穿穴，把浦东浦西紧紧相联；亚洲第一高度的东方明珠广播电视塔，巍峨屹立，光彩夺目；市内郊外一座座高楼大厦拔地而起，一片片市民新居草木葱茏，一条条高架道路越城而过；海内外有识之士纷纷看好上海，中外合作之花盛开浦江两岸；体现群众文化色彩的广场音乐会，不断奏响上海在前进的动人乐曲。在邓小平理论指引下，上海已经站在中国改革开放的前沿，正在发生着划时代的巨变。今日的上海已进入一个崭新的历史阶段。

　　上海是一个充满活力的城市，优越的地理条件，深沉的文化积淀，坚实的经济基础，悠久的中外经济、文化交流历史，形成了这个城市取之不尽的独特资源，也使上海充满勃勃生机。人类社会已经跨入 21 世纪，在新世纪的伟大进程中，上海人民正坚定不移地实施尽快把上海建设成为国际经济、金融、贸易中心和国际航运中心，初步确立国际中心城市地位的发展战略，上海人在创造着更美好的明天，上海这个城市永远年轻。

FOREWORD

Shanghai, a major port city on the west coast of the Pacific, is undergoing the most spectacular growth during its 150-year history as an open port. Its success story is attracting the attention of the world.

Located where the Yangtze River, China's largest river, joins the country's prosperous eastern coast, Shanghai has evolved from a small 19th century fishing town into a modern metropolis and a renowned financial and trade centre in East Asia. The city is the country's largest port with a transportation network extending to China's vast inland regions.

In recent years Shanghai has scored great achievements in its endeavour to become one of the world's economic, financial and trade centres. Since 1990, the city has carried out massive urban reconstruction, and its appearance has kept changing. The new Nanpu, Yangpu and Xupu bridges now span over the Huangpu River. Along with the Oriental Pearl TV Tower and the Jin Mao Tower in Pudong, they form a modern landscape of Shanghai. The three Huangpu River tunnels linking Pudong with Puxi (West Shanghai), a network of elevated highways, mushrooming high-rises, and new residential areas have greatly improved the city's investment environment, attracting a growing number of multinational companies to launch projects in Shanghai. The city has entered a new period of rapid development.

Shanghai is full of vitality. Its superior geographic location, rich cultural heritage, solid economic foundation and a long history of East-West exchanges have all contributed to the city's phenomenal growth. In the 21st Century, the people of Shanghai will continue to work hard to make their city an international banking, trade and shipping centre. The city of Shanghai is forever young.

CONTENTS 目录

城市 新 貌

A NEW LOOK

上海是繁华的城市，发展中的城市，富有朝气的城市。

上海港是东方大港，世界第三。它与世界上160多个国家和地区的400多个港口有运输往来，港口吞吐量雄居世界前列。至2000年末，全市已开辟了通往欧洲、北美、非洲等地的16条国际班轮航线，覆盖世界12个航区。美国、日本等海内外40家著名船舶公司进驻上海港。上海港沿黄浦江绵延深入，两岸高楼耸立，码头缀连，吊车参天，巨轮鸣笛，气势磅礴。上海虹桥和浦东两个国际空港，银鹰翱翔，遨游中华，飞向世界。上海铁路、公路如织，通向四面八方。

有人说，上海长高了。上海曾被誉为"世界建筑博览会"：有仿古典、欧洲皇宫、西班牙、挪威等式花园别墅；有"从苏伊士运河到远东白令海峡最华贵的办公大楼"。但是，当年被称为"远东第一高楼"的国际饭店，也不过是24层。至2000年末，上海超过20层的高层建筑已有1478幢。当年的国际饭店也只能算是小弟弟了。

上海的马路呈棋盘形，大多以全国的省、市、县名命名。随着城市的发展，上海以全新的面貌展现在世人面前。新建成的内环高架路，环绕上海市区，联结浦东浦西，复道行空，绵延47.66公里，其中，浦西段为连续高架道路，全长29.2公里，创造了中国高架道路之最。在市中心，贯通东西、南北的高架路已突兀而起。从上海火车站至梅陇的地铁一号线已延伸到莘庄。从虹桥国际机场至浦东龙东路的地铁二号线一期工程已建成通车。形成了从地面到高空、从地上到地下的现代化交通网络。

Shanghai is a prosperous and dynamic city. Shanghai Port is the country's largest and ranks third in the world in volume of cargo. It has links with more than 400 ports in over 160 countries and regions. By the end of 2000, Shanghai had opened 16 ocean liner routes covering Europe, North America, Asia, Africa and Australia. Meanwhile, 40 major shipping companies from the US, Japan and other countries have set up offices at Shanghai Port. The city's Hongqiao and Pudong international airports can handle nearly 30 million passengers a year. The city is also linked with other Chinese cities by rail and highways.

Known as the "Museum of World Architecture," Shanghai has houses and buildings of classical Chinese, European, Japanese and modern styles. The city has grown taller. The Park Hotel, which was once the highest building in the Far East, is now dwarfed by many new skyscrapers. The city counted 1478 buildings of over 20 stories high at the end of 2000.

The streets of Shanghai are named after Chinese provinces, cities and counties. The elevated Inner Ring Road, 47.66 kilometres long, surrounds the city proper and links Pudong with Puxi. Its Puxi section, a continuous stretch of 29.2 kilometres, is the longest in China. Another elevated highway runs from south to north through the downtown area. The subway Metro Line One connects the Shanghai Railway Station in the north with Xinzhuang in the south, while Metro Line Two links Zhongshan Park in the west with Jinqiao High-Tech Park in Pudong. The newly built light-rail Pearl Line runs from Xinzhuang to Jiangwan. A multi-tiered traffic network has emerged in Shanghai.

上海的城市功能布局正按现代化国际大都市的要求
逐步调整

Shanghai's urban planning is constantly adjusted
to meet the needs of an international metropolis.

上海中央商务区的浦西部分——外滩金融街,也是一个融合了斑斓历史和现代风采的观光胜地

The Bund is both a financial street and tourist attraction, featuring splendid waterfront buildings.

人民广场是上海的公共活动中心,也是浦西市区的巨大"绿肺"

People's Square lies in the heart of Shanghai
and is one of the city's "green lungs"

设施一流，馆藏极丰的上海博物馆新馆1996年10月在人民广场建成开馆
Located in People's Square, the new building of Shanghai Museum was inaugurated in October 1996. It boasts world-class facilities and a vast collection of antiques and art works.

位于东方明珠电视塔内的上海历史发展陈列馆以生动的形式展示上海的开埠与发展
The Shanghai History Museum, housed in the Oriental Pearl TV Tower, provides a vivid display of the city's development.

上海图书馆新馆 1996 年 12 月开馆
The new building of Shanghai Library on Huaihai Road M. was opened to the public in December 1996.

被誉为"中国马戏第一城"的上海马戏城是上海文化旅游新景点。
Shanghai Circus World, claimed to be China best circus theatre, is a new tourist attraction.

上海大剧院的建筑设计和设备配置达到了世界一流水平
Shanghai Grand Theatre features world-advanced architectural designs and facilities.

上海体育场可容纳 8 万名观众
The new Shanghai Stadium can
seat 80,000 spectators.

位于浦东的上海科技城是一座以"自然、人、科技"为主
题的大型综合性科技展馆,总建筑面积为9.65万平方米
Located in Pudong, the Shanghai Science & Technology Museum is a comprehensive museum
on nature, mankind and science. It has a total floor space of 96,500 square metres.

外滩对岸的浦东滨江大道别有一番风光
The beautiful Riverside Avenue faces the Bund across the Huangpu River.

东方明珠广播电视塔是今日上海的标志性新景观之一
The Oriental Pearl TV Tower has become a new landmark of Shanghai.

1991年11月建成通车的南浦大桥是上海市区第一座跨越黄浦江的大桥
The Nanpu Bridge, opened to traffic in November 1991, is the first bridge over the Huangpu River in urban Shanghai.

1993年10月建成通车的杨浦大桥，其主跨径居当时世界同类桥梁之首
Built in October 1993, the Yangpu Bridge has the world's longest central
span for this type of cable－stayed suspension bridge.

延安东路隧道先后建成北线和南线的两个独立通道
The Yan'an Road Tunnel has two one-way tubes for motor traffic.

黄浦江是上海的母亲河，也是上海境内最大的水上通道
The Huangpu River is the mother river of Shanghai
and the largest waterway running through the city.

1997年6月建成通车的徐浦大桥是上海外
环线的组成部分
Constructed in June 1997, the Xupu Bridge
is part of the city qutter Ring Road.

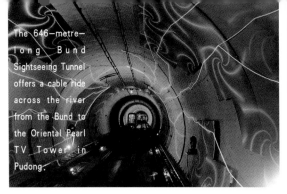

上海外滩观光隧道,隧道长度为646.7米,内径为6.76米,浦东出入口位于东方明珠两侧,浦西出入口位于中山东一路外滩陈毅广场北侧

The 646-metre-long Bund Sightseeing Tunnel offers a cable ride across the river from the Bund to the Oriental Pearl TV Tower in Pudong.

虹桥国际机场的年旅客吞吐量与上海市总人口相近

The Hongqiao International Airport has an annual passenger volume almost equal to the entire population of Shanghai.

轨道交通迅速发展,地铁和明珠线年交通客运量1.36亿人次

Urban rail system is developing fast in Shanghai. The Metro subways and the light-rail Pearl Line can transport 136 million people a year.

上海火车站日均发送旅客达8.2万人次

The Shanghai Railway Station handles an average flow of 82,000 departing passengers every day.

上海开埠以来投资最大的基础设施项目——上海浦东国际机场。
The Pudong International Airport is the city's largest infrastructure undertaking since Shanghai became an open port in 1842.

路立交桥是上海内环线高架路和
路高架路的交点
Caoxi Road Ovepass is the
ing point of the Inner Ring Road
he Humin Highway.

梧桐、油画、庭院灯构成了衡山路的优雅景观
Plane trees, oil paintings and lampposts form
a romantic scenery along Hengshan Road.

小朋友爱与广场鸽为伴
Playing with pigeons in People's Square.

众多公园发挥着平衡市区生态环境的功能
Many downtown parks help improve the
local ecological system.

通过改造铁路上海站周围旧区发展起来的
不夜城商业中心

The Kerry Everbright City is an upstart
commercial centre near the Shanghai Railway
Station.

成熟的投资环境使虹桥经济技术开发区单
位面积吸收的外资数额在各开发区中位居
前茅

The Hongqiao Development Area leads other
economic zones in Shanghai in absorbing
foreign investment, measured by per square
metre.

延中绿地
The Yanzhong Green Area

林荫大道
A tree - covered boulevard
in western Shanghai.

历 史 名 城

A RICH HISTORY

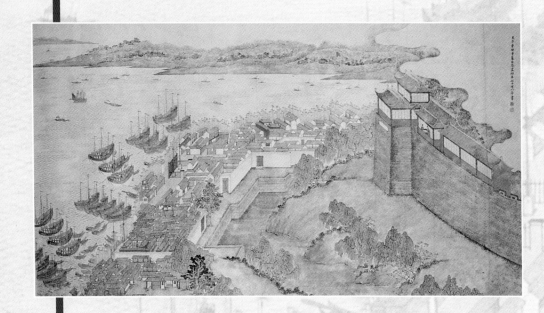

据考古发现，大约在6000年前，上海的先民已在这片土地上生息、劳作、繁衍。春秋时代，这里是吴越的古战场。相传三国东吴孙权曾置青龙战舰于上海的青龙镇，此为东南海上门户。日本圣武朝遣唐使多治比之成一行，曾往返于此港。杜甫有诗曰："吴门转粟帛，泛海陵蓬莱"，记录了青龙镇一时之盛。至宋代，这里有三亭、七塔、十三寺、二十二桥、三十六坊，为东南一巨镇。后因青龙镇港口淤浅，上海黄浦江逐渐兴起。到清代中叶，上海港已成为我国国内外贸易的重要港口。当时，"闽、广、辽、沈之货，鳞萃羽集，远及西洋暹罗之舟，岁也间至，地大物博，号称繁剧，诚江海之通津，东南之都会也"。

上海是中国近代机器工业的发祥地。举其大者，就有江南制造局、轮船招商局、上海机器织布局等。这些企业都开创中国机器工业生产之先。

上海是历史文化名城，留下的历史遗迹甚多。早在西晋时期，著名文学家陆机、陆云就诞生在松江九峰山麓。现在云间九峰的机山和横云山，就是纪念这两位文学家而取的山名。高耸巍峨的龙华塔，相传始建于三国赤乌年间；玲珑古朴的泖塔，始建于唐代，故而又称唐塔；宋代建造的护珠塔，位于天马山中峰，其倾斜度超过了意大利比萨斜塔；宋代建造的兴圣教寺塔（现称"松江方塔"），耸立在松江县城中，呈四方形，被誉为"巍巍楼阙梵王宫"。松江小昆山的北麓有北宋文学家苏轼的遗墨"夕阳在山"。上海西郊乌泥泾有元代女纺织技术家黄道婆的墓址。青浦练塘镇有元代石壁式石桥，结构简洁，环境幽静，富有江南水乡的特色。镇之东南为元代大书法家赵孟𫖯岳父家，故赵之墨迹在上海地区甚多。明清遗址，以园林著称。上海市的豫园建于明代嘉靖年间。园内山石峥嵘，树木苍翠，楼阁参差，"奇秀甲江南"。还有南翔古猗园、嘉定秋霞圃、松江醉白池、青浦曲水园都是明清著名园林。上海是现代化的国际大都市，但是还不失古朴之景。现在，人民路西北的大境阁即是上海在明代所建城墙之一角，经修缮之后，依然保持了它当年的雄姿，为中外游客所青睐。

Archaeological finds indicate that human settlement began here about 6,000 years ago. Shanghai has a written history of over 4,000 years. After the mid-Qing Dynasty, Shanghai became an important port for domestic and foreign trade.

China's modern industry actually originated in Shanghai. The well-known Jiangnan Manufacturing Bureau, the Ship Merchants Co. and the Shanghai Textile Machinery Co. were pioneers of the nation's manufacturing industry.

Shanghai is also the birthplace of the Communist Party of China. The founding of the Party in 1921 is an important event in contemporary Chinese history.

Shanghai is a city with rich cultural heritages. The magnificent Longhua Pagoda dates from 242 AD; the elegant Mao Pagoda was built in the Tang Dynasty (AD 618–907); the Square Pagoda and Huzhu Pagoda — which leans even more than the Tower of Pisa — were both Song Dynasty (960–1279) structures. Loom inventor Huang Daopo and famous Chinese calligrapher Zhao Menfu both lived in Shanghai for some time during the Yuan Dynasty (1206–1368). The city boasts a number of Ming- and Qing-style gardens. The most famous is the Yuyuan Garden, a picturesque compound of pavilions, zigzag corridors, rockery formations, trees, bridges and lotus ponds, built in 1559.

位于青浦区金泽镇的普济
桥建于1265年
Puji Bridge in Jinzhe
Town,Qingpu District was
built in 1265.

位于嘉定区南翔镇的天恩
桥建于明代
Tian'en Bridge in Nanxiang
Town, Jiading District,
dates back to the Ming
Dynasty (1368－1644).

位于松江区的望仙桥建于
宋代
Wangxian Bridge in
Songjiang District dates
from the Song Dynasty
(960-1279).

位于金山区的济渡桥建于
1875年
Jidu Bridge in Jinshan
District was built in 1875.

位于闵行区七宝镇的蒲汇
塘桥建于1518年
Puhuitang Bridge in Qibao
Town, Minhang District,
was constructed in 1518.

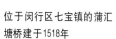

位于青浦区金泽镇的如意
桥建于1261—1294年间
Ruyi Bridge in Jinzhe
Town, Qingpu District, was
constructed between 1261—
1294 during the Yuan
Dynasty.

位于青浦区朱家角镇的放生桥建于1571年，
是上海现存最大的古石拱桥
Built in 1571, Fangshen Bridge in Zhujiajiao
Town, Qingpu District, is the largest arched
stone bridge in Shanghai.

位于松江区天马山上的沪珠塔建于1079年，
塔身倾斜30° 而不倒
Huzhu Pagoda in Songjiang District was
erected in 1079 and is leaning 30 degrees
off the centre.

位于松江区的西林塔建于1265—1274年间，
是上海现存最高的古塔
Xilin Pagoda in Songjiang District, built
between 1265-1274, is the tallest surviving
pagoda in Shanghai.

位于金山区松隐镇的华严塔建于1380年
Huayan Pagoda in Songying Town, Jinshan
District, dates back to 1380.

位于嘉定区的法华塔建于1205—1207年间
Fahua Pagoda in Jiading District was
constructed between 1205 – 1207.

位于松江区的兴圣教寺塔（松江方塔）建于1068年
The Square Pagoda in Songjiang District has stood there since 1068.

嘉定区南翔镇的南翔寺砖塔(双塔)已有千余年历史
Twin Pagodas in Nanxiang Town, Jiading
ct, are over 1,000 years old.

位于青浦区白鹤镇的吉云禅寺塔（青龙塔）建于821年
Black Dragon Pagoda in Baihe Town, Qingpu District,
was constructed in 821.

位于徐汇区龙华镇的龙华塔相传建于242年
Longhua Pagoda in Longhua Town, Xuhui District, was originally built in 242 AD.

位于嘉定区孔庙前的古柏,树龄已有600余年

This cypress in front of the Confucian Temple in Jiading District is more than 600 years old.

位于嘉定区方泰镇的古银杏,树龄已有1200余年,是上海最古老的树木

Planted 1,200 years ago, this gingko tree in Fangtai Town, Jiading District, is the oldest surviving tree in Shanghai.

位于松江区的唐经幢建于859年,是上海地面上最古老的文物

This Stele of Buddhist Scriptures was made in 859 during the Tang Dynasty.

位于嘉定区南翔镇的古猗园始建于1746年
Guqi Garden in Nanxiang Town, Jiading District, was built in 1746.

位于徐汇区华山路的丁香花园为清末名臣李鸿章所建
Qing Dynasty Prime Minister Li Hongzhang was the original owner of the Dingxiang (Lilac) Garden on Huashan Road, Xuhui District.

位于松江区的醉白池始建于1644—1661年间·
Zuibai Pool in Songjiang District was built
between 1644—1661.

位于嘉定区的汇龙潭始建于1588年
Dragons Pond Garden in Jiading District dates back to 1588.

位于青浦区的曲水园始建于1745年
Qushui Garden in Qingpu District was built in 1745.

位于嘉定区的秋霞圃始建于16世纪的初期
Qiuxiapu Garden in Jiading District was
constructed during the mid—16th Century

始建于1559年的豫园是上海的经典景区
Constructed in 1559, Yuyuan Garden is a fine
example of classical Chinese architecture
and landscaping.

❶ 始建于247年的静安寺

❷ 1910年建成的徐家汇天主堂是天主教上海教区主教府所在地

❸ 位于衡山路上的国际礼拜堂

❹ 始建于1882年的玉佛寺供奉有请自缅甸的坐卧玉佛各一尊

❺ 相传始建于242年的龙华寺

❻ 建于1219年的嘉定孔庙设有"仰高"、"兴贤"、"育才"3座牌坊

❼ 建于1341—1368年间的松江清真寺

❽ 位于浦东新区源深路的钦赐仰殿道观

❶ With a history going back to 247 AD, the Jing'an Temple will soon undergo extensive reconstruction.

❷ This Catholic church in Xujiahui was built in 1910.

❸ The Community Church on Hengshan Road.

❹ The Jade Buddha Temple was built in 1882 to house two jade statues of Buddha from Burma.

❺ Founed in 242 AD, the Longhua temple.

❻ The Confucian Temple in Jiading District was built in 1219. It has three decorative archways.

❼ This mosque in Songjiang County was built between 1341—1368.

❽ A centuries—old Taoist temple on Yuanshen Road in Pudong.

上海素有"世界建筑博览会"之美誉,风格迥异的各国建筑是城市发展的缩影,历史风云的见证。

Shanghai is known as the "museum of world architecture". Buildings of different styles and periods can be found in the city.

孙中山(1866—1925,中国伟大的革命先行者)故居
The former residence of Sun Yat－sen (1866
－1925), founder of the Republic of China.

宋庆龄 (1893—1981,孙中山夫人、中国的领导人之一) 故居
The former residence of Soong Ching Ling, widow of Sun Yat-sen
and honorary Chinese president until her death in 1981.

韬奋(1895—1944,中国著名记者)故居
The residence of Zou Taofeng (1895 － 1944),
a well known Chinese journalist and publisher.

黄炎培(1878—1965,中国著名政治家)故居
The former home of Huang Yanpei (1878 －
1965), a Chinese educator and politician.

鲁迅(1881—1936,中国著名文学家)故居
The former residence of Lu Xun (1881 －
1936), a famous Chinese writer.

中国共产党第一次全国代表大会会址
The venue of the First National Congress of
the Communist Party of China in July 1921.

人民生活
THE PEOPLE

上海是个移民城市。上海市民的先辈来自全国的四面八方。在市中心，有95%的居民是外地籍人口。

上海民居多为石库门建筑，这些房屋用石条砌门框，有两扇乌漆大门和铜门环，内有东西厢房、前楼、后楼、亭子间等。一屋可以多用，一楼可住多家，适合大城市人口集中、土地紧张的需要。现在，很多上海人已迁入了高层或多层的居民小区。那里，房屋整齐、卫生、煤气等设施齐全，阳光充足，绿树成荫，环境幽静。由于居住条件的变化，市民的生活方式和心态也随之发生变化。

上海是快节奏社会。作为国际大都市，上海经济比较发达，信息敏捷，同时，竞争比较激烈。各类证券市场，期货交易市场行情多变。加上地域较大，人口集中，市内交通繁忙，市民上班下班出外办事都讲究时间观念。

上海是中外文化的交汇地，接受现代化的教育比较早。因此，上海人的科技、文化水平比较高，拥有一大批全国著名的学者、专家、教授，以及人数众多的技术熟练工人。

上海人开放好学。现在，上海人中间流行一句话："为了您的将来，抓紧学习。"上海有许多开风气之先的新鲜事。如在公园、街头出现的"英语角"，参加的人有老人，有孩子，年青人更多，大家围在一起用英语对话，以此提高外语对话能力。又如，社会上出现"电脑热"。到2000年底，累计275万人报名参加包括12个项目的计算机等级考试，其中159万人获得优秀或合格证书。每当夜幕降临，教室内灯火通明，校门外自行车成排，一批批莘莘学子，刻苦求学。全市出现了一股"学知识、学科学、学技术"的热潮，参加各种业余学习的人数超过了360万人次。

上海人的生活丰富多彩，业余爱好因人而异。既有东方情调，又受外来文化的影响。每天清晨，在公园林荫绿化地带可以看到操练太极拳和跳迪斯科舞的人群能自然地融合在一起。在娱乐场所，既有酷爱中国传统戏曲的戏迷，也有欣赏西方音乐，热爱华尔兹舞，沉湎梵婀铃琴下的人们。上海的民俗既保留了春节、端午、中秋、重阳等传统节日，也有异国情调的活动。

Shanghai is a city of migrants. The early settlers came from many parts of China. About 95 per cent of the urban population are not natives by origin.

In the old downtown area, many families still live in "Shikumen" or alley houses with stone-framed gates, built in the early 20th century. Many of these alley houses are shared by several households. But in recent years, more and more downtown residents have moved to high-rise apartments. Improved housing conditions have started to change Shanghai people's way of life.

Although life in Shanghai is fast paced, local people are used to the hustle and bustle. The local market is brisk and competition is fierce. A large number of Shanghai people are stockholders.

The city is not only an industrial base, but also a base for scientific and technological research. It boasts many first-rate universities, research institutes, renowned scientists and skilled professionals. There are also many evening schools and adult colleges for people who are eager to learn. The number of people with certificates in computer education had increased to 1.59 million in 2000.

Life is colourful in Shanghai. In the morning people start their day doing Tai Chi, fan dance and other exercises in the parks; during the day, senior citizens gather at the teahouse to enjoy ballad singing or Chinese opera; and after dark disco clubs are thronged with young people. The city clings to old traditions but also absorbs foreign influences. As a result, Christmas and other Western holidays are celebrated as much as the Spring Festival and the Mid-Autumn Festival.

上海居民的平均期望寿命已上升到
男性76.71岁、女性80.8岁
Shanghai's life expectancy at birth
has reached 76.71 for men and 80.8
for women.

热爱运动的上海人
Shanghai people like outdoor activities.

每周五天工作制使上海市民有了更多的休闲时间
The five-day work week, introduced in 1995, has
enabled local citizens to have more leisure time.

移动通信设备已广泛进入市民生活
Mobile phones are common these days.

A young woman posts application letters in
hopes of landing a good job.

业余时装模特儿们
"Amateur fashion models."

传统食品仍有市场潜力
Traditional food products are still popular.

至2000年末全市连锁商业网点已达
4460多家
The number of chain stores exceeded
4,460 in Shanghai in 2000.

"菜篮子"工程的产业化、市场化水平进一步提高
The city's "Basket Project" has led to
an abundant supply of vegetables.

市民外出就餐次数的增多使餐饮业频获商机
More and more Shanghainese like to dine out,
giving a boost to local catering business.

上海是我国商品花卉生产和销售
的主要基地之一

Shanghai is a big producer and
consumer of fresh flowers.

富于投资意识和风险意识的上海人
对证券市场及外汇市场的任何波动
都很敏感

Many people in Shanghai are
investing in stocks and are
sensitive to market fluctuations.

最近开发的多伦路文
化名人街融旅游与购
物于一体,吸引着众
多的中外游人。
Duolun Road, home to
many of China's writers
and cultural celebrities,
has been renovated as
a shopping and
sightseeing street.

青年消费者为商业步
行街带来强劲购买力
Young consumers are
the driving force of
local retail business.

上海人的居住条件日益改善,至2000年末
市区人均居住面积达11.8平方米
The housing condition is steadily improving in
Shanghai with per capita floor space reaching
11.8 square metres for urban families.

骑车上
The morning rus

成人仪式让年满18岁的青年感悟到人生的使命
Young people take the "citizenship oath"
when they reach the age of 18.

上海是一本巨大的爱情诗集,每时每刻都在
产生新的诗句

Shanghai is a city full of romance. Many
weddings take place every day.

郊县艺术节
A folk art festival in a suburban town of Shanghai.

龙舟表演
A dragon boat race.

载歌载舞，自娱自乐
Crowds in front of Peking opera masks.

京剧小票友
Young fans of Peking opera.

"待会儿看我们露一手！"
Off the stage.

72

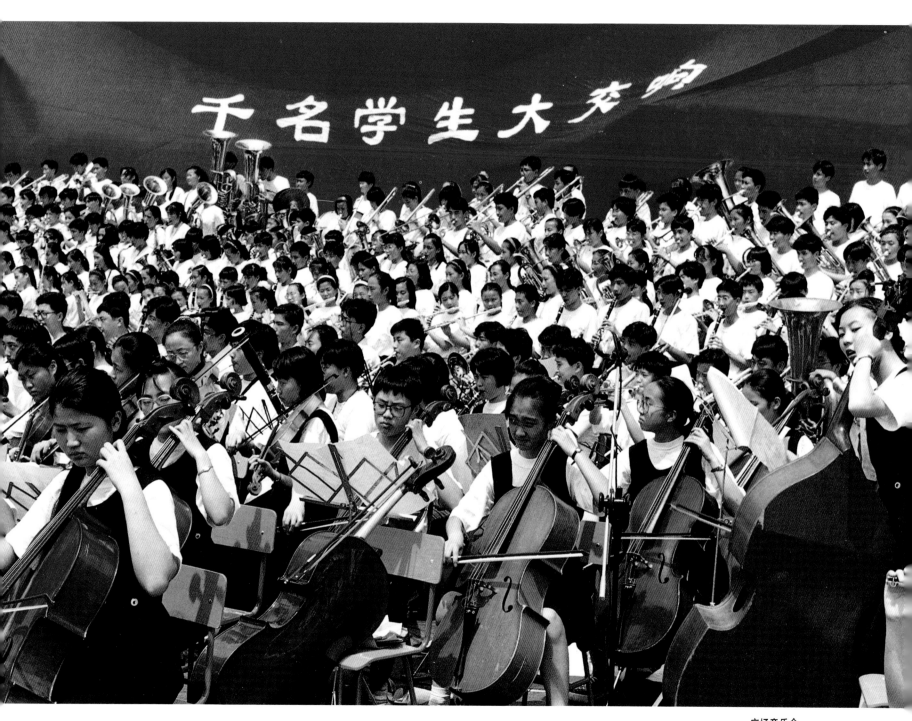

广场音乐会
An open-air concert by Shanghai students.

上海60岁以上的老年人已占全市
人口的18%,他们的生活状况受到
全社会的关心

People aged over 60 now make up
18 per cent of the city's population.
Their well‑being has become a
focus of social concern.

农家女
A village girl

三代情
A happy family

水乡一景
Ancient town

刺绣工艺
Silk embroidery
is a local tradition.

剪纸小能手
A young hand
in paper-cutting

元宵灯会
The Lantern Festival

舞龙
Dragon dance

农民画家创作不离
Peasant artists paint from

网络酒吧吸引了许多热衷"网上冲浪"的年青人
Cyber cafe has become a vogue among many
young people.

自己动手做陶器，乐趣无穷
What fun!

具情调的小书店
cozy bookstore

来一杯果汁，来一点好心情
Chatting over fruit juice.

太阳岛等郊县一批新建的旅游景
点成为市民休闲度假的好去处。
SunIsland is one of the many holiday
resorts built in the suburbs in recent
years.

久居都市的人们格外亲水,节假日
的水上乐园总是人满为患
The water parks are a big draw in
summer for urban residents,
especially children.

各种形式的现代装置艺术颇受市民赏识
Modern art finds rich soil in Shanghai.

又一批富于冒险精神的上海人在上海中国旅
行社的组织下前往新疆罗布泊荒漠探险旅游
These Shanghai people embark on an adventure
tour of Lop Nur, a desert in northwest Xinjiang.

越来越多的上海人自费赴境外旅游
More and More local Chinese now
travel overseas at their own expense.

来自全国各地的游客在上海受到热情欢迎

Visitors from ethnic minority areas.

经济建设

ECONOMIC PROGRESS

上海是中国的老工业基地，在改革开放中，再现辉煌。2000年上海国内生产总值GDP总量超过4551.15亿元人民币，人均GDP达到4180美元。现在，上海已确立了6大支柱产业：信息、金融、商贸、汽车、成套设备、房地产。2000年上海轿车产量突破了25万辆。上海钢和钢材产量居全国钢铁工业第一位。通信产业五大类产品，包括程控交换机、光纤通信、移动电话、卫星通信和终端通信等销售收入甚为可观。上海还拥有中国最大的现代化石油炼制、石油化工、合成纤维和新型塑料的联合生产企业。

上海第三产业在国民生产总值中的比重逐年提高。重点发展金融保险、商业贸易、房地产、旅游、服务、信息咨询等产业，形成了大流通、大贸易、大市场的格局。商品、金属、粮油、航运、证券等各类交易所、外汇交易中心、外国银行、保险公司、财务公司等纷纷"抢滩"，上海已成为中国内外资金融机构种类、数量最多的城市之一。

上海多元化、多层次、多渠道的大外贸格局已臻雏型。目前上海已与214个国家和地区的客商建立了贸易联系。2000年上海口岸进出口商品总额1093.1亿美元，占全国的近四分之一（23%）。

上海已成为外商投资的热土。至2000年末，上海累计签订吸收外资合同项目2.79万项，合同金额942.85亿美元，其中，直接吸收外资合同项目2.23万项，合同金额454.23亿美元。至2000年末，世界500强跨国公司中，有一半以上在上海投资。其中，落户浦东的超过100家。

上海农村城郊型现代化农业格局正在形成，"菜篮子工程"取得了显著成效。农村城市化步伐也大大加快。

Shanghai is one of China's old industrial bases. The reform over the past 20 years has injected the city with new vitality. In 2000, the city's GDP exceeded 455.1 billion yuan (US$55 billion) with the per capita GDP reaching US$4180. Information technology, finance, trade, automobile, machinery and real estate industries have become the six pillars of Shanghai's economy. The city produced 250,000 cars in 2000, while its steel output is the biggest in the country. The city also has the nation's largest petrochemical complex.

The service industry now represents a growing part of Shanghai's GDP, with emphasis on the development of finance, insurance, commerce, real estate and tourism sectors. The Shanghai Stock Exchange and various specialised markets have developed rapidly in the city, which also hosts the country's Foreign Exchange Trading System and a large number of foreign banks, insurance companies and accounting firms.

Shanghai has fostered trade relations with 214 countries and regions. Its gross value of imports and exports in 2000 surpassed US$109.31 billion, accounting for 23 per cent of the national total.

By the end of 2000, the city had attracted more than 27,900 foreign investment projects, involving US$94.28 billion in capital money. Of which, 22,300 are direct foreign investment projects, involving US$45.42 billion. More than half of the world's Top 500 multinational companies have invested in Shanghai. Many are located in Pudong.

Modern farming is emerging in suburban Shanghai. The government-supported "Basket Project" has proven successful in enriching local food supplies. Meanwhile, urbanisation is benefiting the rural families in suburban Shanghai.

新老商业建筑同为
"中华商业第一街"南
京路步行街增辉
China's No.1 shopping
sreet — Nanjing Road.

空间开阔、绿地成片的徐家汇商城已成为上海商业发展最快的地区之一
Xujiahui – a fast growing commercial hub in southwest Shanghai.

璀璨的商海明珠—上海豫园商城
The Yuyuan Tourist Mall is both a
shopping hub and a sightseeing
spot in the old town area.

在消费品买方市场基本形成的情况下,上海商业加速调整业态结构、商品结构和网点布局
Shanghai has changed from the sellers' market to the buyers' market. Department
stores and chain stores opened one after another.

全国和世界各地的商品在上海这个大市场中集散、流通
Shanghai is a large distribution centre of domestic and foreign consumer goods.

至2000年末进入上海的外资经营性金融机构已有66家,其中获准经营人民币业务的外资银行已达25家。全市有21家在沪外资银行被其总行确定为中国境内业务的主报告行

By the end of 2000, 66 foreign banks and financial institutions had opened branches in Shanghai, and 25 banks are allowed to do Renminbi business.

2000年上海证券市场各类证券成交额达4.99万亿元人民币,其中股票成交3.14万亿元人民币。图为上海证券交易所交易大厅

The new building of Shanghai Stock Exchange, where securities trading totalled 4,990 billion yuan (US$603 billion) in 2000.

浦东外高桥保税区转口贸易活跃,外向功能进一步强化。

The Waigaoqiao Free Trade Zone has many Chinese and foreign companies engaged in entrepot trade.

至2000年末浦东陆家嘴金融贸易区已建成289幢现代化楼宇,其中商办楼宇112幢,中外金融机构、国内外大集团总部,各类要素市场加快向这里集聚

The number of modern buildings in Pudong Lujiazui business district reached 289 in 2000, attracting many multinational companies to move their regional headquarters there.

上海的钢铁制造业通过产品结构、生产布局的调整,向精品基地方向发展
A view of the Baoshan Iron and Steel Complex.

2000年上海口岸的国际标准集装箱吞吐量已达561.2万标准箱,在国际集装箱运输业中的排名已提升为第六位
Shanghai Port handled 5.61 million TEU containers in 2000, ranking 6th in the world.

上海生产的电站成套设备销售额在全国市场连年居首位

Shanghai is the largest supplier of power generating equipment in China.

上海航天局研制的长征系列运载火箭

The Long March carrier rockets are developed and manufactured by the Shanghai Aerospace Industry Bureau.

上海航空公司的运能和航线辐射面逐年扩大
Shanghai Airlines' fleet and routes are expanding every year.

上海制造的民用客机
A jet plane is being assembled at
the Shanghai Aircraft Company.

上海最大中美合资企业上海通用汽车公司生产的第一辆别克轿车下线
The first Buick sedan rolls off the production line of Shanghai General Motors
in Pudong-the largest Sino-US joint venture in the city.

上海的石油化工及精细化工工业在降低物耗和能耗的同时提高了产量和质量
The Jinshan Petrochemical Complex has managed to improve efficiency by cutting the cost of energy and materials.

❶ 上海造船工业追求高科技含量和高附加值
❷ 上海电话网实现8位拨号,为信息港建设打开了空间
❸ 浦东孙桥现代农业开发区的智能型蔬菜温室
❹ 2000年上海高新技术产业产值占全市工业总产值的
　比重达到20.6%
❺ 上海生产的东海家用电脑市场占有率不断提高
❻ 上海有重点地强化应用技术的开发、中试和推广,促进产品
　的创新和升级

● High-tech, high value-added vessels are the goal of the city's shipbuilding industry.

● The switch to eight-digit dialing numbers has opened up more space for the expansion of the city's telecommunications sector.

● A computer-programmed greenhouse farm in the Sunqiao Modern Agriculture Zone.

● Hi-tech enterprises contributed 20.6 per cent of the city's industrial output in 2000.

● Shanghai-made Donghai personal computers enjoy a growing market share.

● The city supports the development of new technology to upgrade local products.

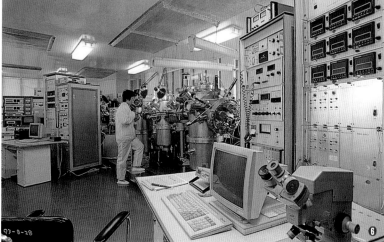

社会发展
SOCIAL DEVELOPMENT

"日月光华·旦复旦兮",此语也是上海复旦大学校名的寓意,表达了追求光明、振兴教育的意义。这所世界著名大学已有90年的历史,与它同时代诞生的上海交通大学(原名南洋公学)、同济大学、圣约翰大学、沪江大学等,有的正在建设成为世界一流大学,有的虽已改名,也是生气勃勃,焕发了青春。建国后,还新建了一批现代化的新型大学。至2000年末全市高等院校有37所,中学861所,小学1021所,以及成人高校37所。上海还有一批特殊学校如盲童学校和为外国儿童就读的国际学校等。

海派文化是具有上海地方特征的文化。兼容并蓄、海纳百川是它的特点,上海拥有一大批文艺演出团体和著名的导演和演员。剧种有京剧、昆剧、沪剧、越剧、淮剧、音乐、舞蹈、话剧、滑稽、评弹等。影视荧屏节目丰富多彩。上海有2个广播电台、5个电视台、4个电影制片厂和良好的拍摄基地。

上海是世界的舞台,全国以及世界著名的演员、艺术家都来这里表演。上海每两年举办一次电视节。每届电视节有世界几十个国家和地区前来参映和观摩。中国上海国际艺术节每年举办一次,各兄弟省市和国外的著名剧团以最新最好的剧目前来参演。上海举办的国际电影节,汇集了当今世界电影文化的潮流,属于世界A级电影节。

上海还有许多具有地方特色和文化气息很浓的节日,如上海旅游节、徐汇桂花节、南汇桃花节、奉贤风筝节、闸北茶文化节、普陀花卉节等。为上海人所喜爱的外滩、徐家汇、复兴公园等地的广场文化,也是上海的一大文化景观。

上海的福州路是著名的"文化街",一条长500米的街聚集百余家书屋报馆。现在福州路仍然保持了文化街的特色。一座现代化的上海书城已经正式建成。至2000年末,上海有图书出版社35家,年出版图书12682种。公开发行的报纸有103种,期刊613种。

上海近年来,每年都取得2000项左右的重大科技成果。这些成果中约有三分之一达到或接近国际水平。人工合成酵母丙氨转移核糖核酸、1.56米天体测量望远镜、长征四号运载火箭、30万千瓦核电站、世界最大跨径叠合梁斜拉桥等一大批高水平成果问世。

上海已拥有一批标志性的文化设施。如黄浦江畔的东方明珠广播电视塔,南京路上的国际广播新闻中心,人民广场中心的上海博物馆、上海大剧院,淮海中路上的上海图书馆等。上海正在建设与一流城市相适应的一流文化。

Shanghai has 37 institutions of higher learning, 861 secondary schools, 1021 elementary schools, and 37 adult universities. It also has special schools for the handicapped and 25 international schools.

Shanghai is a big melting pot with a population largely made up of migrants. This has contributed to the city's unique culture. Shanghai boasts a large number of celebrated artists, directors and performing troupes. It has two radio stations, five television stations, four film studios and several filming parks.

Many world-class musicians and artists have come to perform in Shanghai. The city regularly holds international TV, film and art festivals, drawing well-known artists and companies from around the world and bringing an abundance of high-quality programmes to Shanghai audiences.

Other popular cultural events include Shanghai Tourism Festival, Xuhui Osmanthus Festival, Nanhui Peach Blossom Festival, Fengxian Kite-flying Festival, Zhabei Tea Culture Festival and Putuo Horticulture Festival. Open-air concerts and performances on the Bund and other public squares also help to enliven the city life. Fuzhou Road, known as the "Cultural Street," is 500 meters long and lined with bookstores and publishing houses, including the Shanghai Book City — a giant book retailer in a modern building. In 2000, the city's 35 publishing companies released 12,682 titles of books. Meanwhile, 103 newspapers and 613 journals are published locally.

Every year, some 2,000 scientific discoveries and technological breakthroughs are made in Shanghai, nearly one-third of which are considered to be at the world's advanced level.

Shanghai boasts many new cultural landmarks, such as the Oriental Pearl TV Tower, Shanghai Grand Theatre, Shanghai Museum, Shanghai Library and Shanghai Science & Technology Museum.

上海影城
Shanghai Film Art Centre

上海广播电视国际新闻交流中心
Shanghai International Radio &
TV Exchange Centre.

上海展览中心
Shanghai Exhibition Centre

上海音乐厅
Shanghai Concert Hall

上海的文艺舞台不断涌现有影响的精品佳作

Colourful stages in Shangh

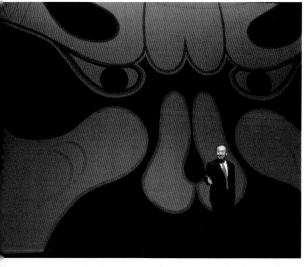

创意新颖的城市雕塑引发人们丰富的遐想
Graceful and innovative urban sculptures are
seen everywhere.

全民健身运动蓬勃开展
A massive turnout of runners. The city is full of sports enthusiasts.

上海运动员在国内国
际大赛中屡获殊荣

Shanghai athletes have
captured many gold medals
in national and international
competitions.

孜孜不倦
All carried away...

毕业前夕
Graduation day

大学校园
Fudan University

夜自修
Campus at night

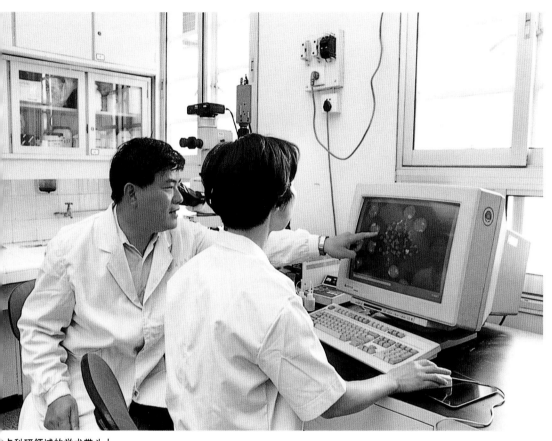

点科研领域的学术带头人
cientists in genetic engineering.

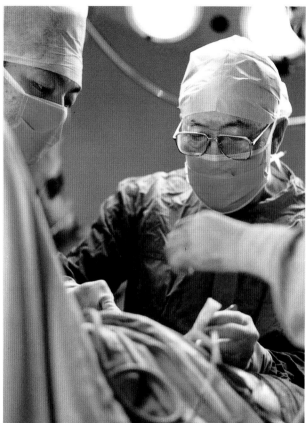

模范医学专家吴孟超
Wu Mengchao, a well known Shanghai doctor.

全市学龄儿童入学率达到99.9%
The enrollment rate of school-age children in Shanghai has
reached 99.9 per cent.

到福利院抱一抱孤儿,让他们享受到普通家庭的亲情
These people visit the Shanghai Children's Welfare Institute
to hug and talk to the orphans and let them feel family love.

癌症患者俱乐部的成员欢度"5岁"生日
These cancer patients hold a birthday party
for one of their club members.

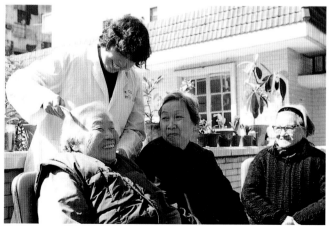

敬老院温暖如家
As warm as home. The scene of a local
senior citizens' home.

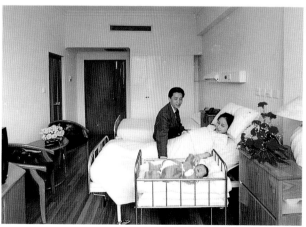

2000年上海户籍人口出生率为5.3‰，死亡率7.2‰，自然增长率为−1.9‰。创建爱婴医院、爱婴区县的工作促进了母婴保健水平的提高
The birth rate of permanent Shanghai residents was 5.3 per thousand in 2000, while mortality rate was 7.2 per thousand. Most maternity hospitals have adopted modern nursing methods.

慈善募捐得到热烈响应
Charity fund-raising attracts young donors.

社会服务志愿者在行动
Volunteers in action.

求职觅才上市场
A crowded job market.

下岗女工在接受电脑培训
Laid-off textile workers get training in computer applications.

对 外 交 往
INTERNATIONAL EXCHANGE

上海是国际大都市，对外交流活动频繁，朋友遍天下。到上海访问的有许多国家元首政要，世界著名的金融家、实业家、专家学者、艺术大师，还有不同肤色的来上海求学的莘莘学子和观光旅游者。中国有句古话："有朋自远方来，不亦乐乎。"上海人民热烈欢迎各方来客，开展各项交流活动。同时，上海也派出各类艺术、经贸和学术团体出访世界各国，进行经济、文化交流活动。

上海在开展对外交流活动中，增进了与世界各国的友谊，加深了彼此的了解，上海与各国的友好关系更为密切。至 2000 年末，上海已与 39 个国家的 47 个城市（省、州、区）结成友好城市或建立了长期友好交流关系，上海有各国驻沪领事馆 39 个，驻沪新闻机构 46 家，外资金融机构 66 家，外资金融机构驻沪代表处 166 家。更有许多外国企业家来上海投资，参加各类经济活动。在第 11 届华东商品交易会上，有来自五大洲 125 个国家（地区）的 10562 名客商参加。到上海参加上海市市长国际企业家咨询会的成员，都是世界有影响的企业家和经济学家。

在上海的荧屏、舞台上也频频有世界顶级艺术团体、著名艺术家亮相，展现各国艺术家的风采。

让世界了解上海，上海也要了解世界。沟通上海与世界各国的"桥梁"，日臻发达。上海的民航已与 20 多个国家（地区）的 64 个城市通航。邮电通信方面，上海与 195 个国家（地区）建立了国际特快专递业务。上海国际长途电话已实现全球通，长途电话可通世界各国。上海还有许多促进对外交流的"无形桥梁"，那就是上海与世界各国人民的文化艺术交流活动。每年上海都要举办各类国际性的节庆活动，如"中国上海国际艺术节"等，上海为世界一流的文化艺术提供了舞台，也充分展示了上海独特的文化和迷人的风采。

上海欢迎你们，期待着有更多国外朋友到上海来作客。

Shanghai is an international metropolis with a lot of conferences, symposiums, fairs and festivals. The city has received many foreign heads of state, business leaders, scholars, artists, and a vast number of tourists. Meanwhile, it also sends out its own business, academic and art delegations abroad to participate in various exchange activities.

International exchanges have promoted Shanghai to the outside world. By the end of 2000, the city had established sister-city relationships with 47 cities in 39 countries. Thirty-nine foreign countries have opened consulates in Shanghai; 46 foreign news organisations have local bureaux; 66 foreign financial institutions have local branches and another 166 have representative offices. During the 11th East China Trade Fair held in 2000, 10,562 businesspeople from 125 countries and regions came looking for deals or business partners. The International Business Leaders' Advisory Council for Shanghai Mayor is a gathering of the world's influential business leaders and economists.

Internationally famous art troupes frequently appear on local stages, and Shanghai cinemas and televisions often show imported films and TV programmes. The hosting of many international festivals has made Shanghai a stage for world-class performances.

① 上海国际少年儿童文化艺术节
② 上海国际电影节
③ 上海国际茶文化节
④ 上海国际电视节
⑤ 上海国际服装文化节
⑥ 上海国际魔术节
⑦ 上海国际广播音乐节
⑧ 上海国际花卉节
⑨ 中国上海国际艺术节

① Shanghai International Children's Art Festival
② Shanghai International Film Festival
③ Shanghai International Tea Festival
④ Shanghai International TV Festival
⑤ Shanghai International Fashion Festival
⑥ Shanghai International Festival of Magic
⑦ Shanghai International Broadcast & Music Festival
⑧ Shanghai International Flower Festival
⑨ Shanghai International Festival of Arts, China

"上海合作组织"成员国元首会议2001年6月在上海举行
The presidents of the six member countries of the Shanghai
Co-operation Organisation held a summit meeting in June 2001.

上海改革开放取得的巨大成就引起国际社会浓厚兴趣，各国政要
大多将上海作为访华的必到之地
Shanghai's enormous success in reform and opening has captured
the world attention. Most foreign heads of state and government
leaders would make a stop in Shanghai while visiting China.

美国总统比尔·克林顿及家人在上海(1998年6月)
Then US President Bill Clinton and his family visited Shanghai in June 1998.

为上海发展作出突出贡献的境外人士荣获"上海市荣誉市民"称号
Foreigners who have made outstanding contribution to the development of Shanghai are awarded the title of "Honorary Shanghai Citizen".

上海市市长国际企业家咨询会议的成员会间小憩
Participants of the International Business Leaders' Advisory Council for The Mayor of Shanghai talk with Mayor Xu Kuangdi (right).

在上海工作、学习、旅游的外国人日益增多，
这座开放型的城市令他们倍感亲切

Shanghai is becoming an international city and
the number of foreigners working, studying
and travelling in Shanghai is rapidly increasing.

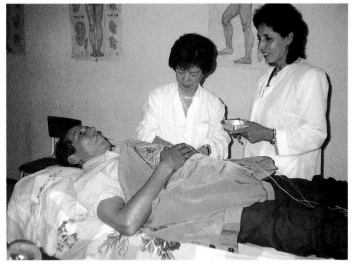

在上海的外国人也能看到世界上大型的演出

Foreigners in Shanghai have the chance to see world-famous performances.

至2000年末上海开办了25所面向境外人士子女的国际学校

By the end of 2000, the city has opened 25 international
schools for the children of local expats.

上海努力增进各国人民对自己的了解。图为中加两国领导人为在加拿大举行的上海摄影展剪彩

Shanghai is keen to promote itself to the outside world. Chinese and Canadian leaders cut ribbon at the opening of the Shanghai Photo Exhibition in Canada.

上海市人民政府新闻办公室编   COMPILED BY THE INFORMATION OFFICE OF SHANGHAI MUNICIPALITY

顾　问	王仲伟			
主　编	焦　扬			
编委	王建军	李伟国	夏　艺	
	陈志强	鲍克怡	王　岳	
特约编辑	谢新发	王石泉	秦丽萍	
撰　文	吴永甫	周　竞		
翻　译	王宁军	荣新民		
装帧设计	赵松华	洪丽诗		
封面书法	邓　明			
摄　影	谢新发	达向群	欧阳鹤	纪海鹰
	徐裕根	潘文龙	陈志民	陈石麟
	郭一江	杭凌冰	荣牧民	沈　良
	赵中华	陈　盛	金定根	殷增善
	阎维祥	吕毅民	杨溥涛	张国威
	丁　盛	丁志平	大田大右	王庆宏
	方忠麟	史兴忠	叶明训	丛名正
	刘炳源	许志刚	刘延平	余洪明
	邹　桓	何伟铭	何香生	汪启昀
	忻正伯	陈仁群	陈光时	陈启宇
	陈春轩	陈康龄	邵黎阳	杨中俭
	杨光亮	杨建正	金宝源	竺　钢
	张　郇	张　潮	张其正	张雪雄
	祖忠人	姚元祥	夏本建	高　原
	高　峰	唐载清	崔佳德	蔡旭洲
	臧志成	黄田宝	焦　扬	邢　俊
	姚　倬	许根顺	楼文彪	胡宝平

上 海 辞 书 出 版 社 出 版

责任编辑	于鹏彬	徐福荣
摄影编辑	谢新发	
美术编辑	汪　溪	
封面设计	姜　明	

ADVISER   Wang Zhongwei

EDITOR IN CHIEF   Jiao Yang

MEMBERS OF THE EDITORIALBOARD   Wang Jianjun, Li Weiguo, Xia Yi, Chen Zhiqiang, Bao Keyi, Wang Yue

SPECIAL COPY EDITORS   Xie Xinfa, Wang Shiquan, Qin Liping

WRITERS   Wu Yongfu, Zhou Jing

TRANSLATORS   Wang Ningjun, Rong Xinmin

GRAPHIC DESIGNERS   Zhao Songhua, Hong Lishi

FRONT COVER CALLIGRAPHY   Deng Ming

PHOTOGRAPHERS   Xie Xinfa, Da Xiangqun, Ouyang He, Ji Haiying, Xu Yugen, Pan Wenlong, Chen Zhimin, Chen Shilin, Guo Yijiang, Hang Linbing, Rong Mumin, Shen Liang, Zhao Zhonghua, Chen Sheng, Jin Dinggen, Yin Zengshan, Yan Weixiang, Lu Yimin, Yang Putao, Zhang Guowei, Ding Sheng, Ding Zhiping, Datian Dayou, Wang Qinghong, Fang Zhonglin, Shi Xingzhong, Ye Mingxun, Cong Mingzheng, Liu Bingyuan, Xu Zhigang, Liu Yanping, Yu Hongmin, Zou Huan, He Weiming, He Xiangsheng, Wang Qiyun, Xin Zhengbo, Chen Renqun, Chen Guangshi, Chen Qiyu, Chen Chunxuan, Chen Kangling, Shao Liyang, Yang Zhongjian, Yang Guangliang, Yang Jianzheng, Jin Baoyuan, Zhu Gang, Zhang Xun, Zhang Chao, Zhang Qizheng, Zhang Xuexiong, Zu Zhongren, Yao Yuanxiang, Xia Benjian, Gao Yuan, Gao Feng, Tang Zaiqing, Cui Jiade, Cai Xuzhou, Zang Zhicheng, Huang Tianbao, Jiao Yang, Xing Jun, Yao Zhuo, Xu Genshun, Lou Wenbiao, Hu Baoping

PUBLISHED BY SHANGHAI LEXICOGRAPHIC PUBLISHING HOUSE

CHIEF COPYEDITORS   Yu Pengbin, Xu Furong

PHOTO EDITOR   Xie Xinfa

ART DESIGN   Wang Xi

COVER DESIGN   Jiang Ming

上 海（第三版） 上海辞书出版社出版　上海陕西北路457号　邮政编码：200040　上海辞书出版社发行所发行　深圳中华商务联合印刷有限公司印刷

开本787×1092　1/12　印张11　2001年8月第3版　2001年8月第1次印刷　ISBN 7-5326-0816-6/F·55　定价：精装108元

SHANGHAI (3rd Edition) Published by the SHANGHAI PUBULISHING HOUSE, 457 Shanxi Road N, Shanghai 200040 Distributed by the SHANGHAI LEXICOGRAPHIC PUBLISHING HOUSE

Printed   by   Shenzhen C&C Joint Printing Co. Ltd.   ISBN 7-5326-0816-6/F·55   Price: 108 yuan (hard-cover)

图书在版编目（CIP）数据

上海/上海市人民政府新闻办主编. ——3版.——上海：上海辞书出版社，2001.9

ISBN 7-5326-0816-6

I. 上… II. 上… III. 上海市—概况　IV. K925.1

中国版本图书馆CIP数据核字（2001）第057526号